WONDER ✳ CABINET

WONDER

CABINET

DAVID BARBER

TRIQUARTERLY BOOKS
NORTHWESTERN UNIVERSITY PRESS
Evanston, Illinois

TriQuarterly Books
Northwestern University Press
www.nupress.northwestern.edu

Printed in the United States of America

10   9   8   7   6   5   4   3   2   1

ISBN 0-8101-5172-3 (cloth)
ISBN 0-8101-5173-1 (paper)

Library of Congress Cataloging-in-Publication Data

Barber, David, date.
  Wonder cabinet / David Barber.
    p. cm.
  Poems.
  Includes bibliographical references.
    ISBN 0-8101-5172-3 (cloth : alk. paper) — ISBN
  0-8101-5173-1 (pbk. : alk. paper)
    I. Title.
  PS3552.A59194W66 2006
  811.54—dc22
                                    2005035080

For my family
And for Peter Davison, in memoriam

Nature loves to hide itself.
Heraclitus

The world of dew is the world of dew. And yet, and yet.
Issa

CONTENTS

ACKNOWLEDGMENTS

My thanks to the editors of the journals where the following poems, sometimes in earlier versions, first appeared: *Arts & Letters* ("Masters of the Florilegium," third section of "From a Burbank Catalogue" [as "Handkerchiefs on the Lawn"]); *Atlantic Monthly* ("Pilgrim's Progress," "Tar Pit," "Bambino Sutra," "Thumbnail Sketch of the Tulipmania"); *Euphony* ("Cautionary Tale"); *Field* ("Houdini Sutra"); *Gettysburg Review* ("Procrustean"); *Michigan Quarterly Review* ("Pathetic Fallacy"); *Nebraska Review* ("Source," "Funicular," "Horse Chestnuts," "Sympathy for the Mapinguari," "Aphrodite's Mousetrap"); *New Criterion* ("Rogue Moss," "Psalm for a Sugarhouse"); *New England Review* (first section of "From a Burbank Catalogue" [as "Burbank's Thornless"]); *New Republic* ("Matchbook Hymn"); *Parnassus* ("A Colonial Epitaph Annotated," "Inquest"); *Ploughshares* ("Shades of Alexandria"); *Poetry* ("Great Stone Face Sutra," "Double Elephant Folio Sutra," "To the Trespasser"); *Shenandoah* ("Ode to William Wells," "Calenture"); *Slate* ("Lullaby in Steerage," "Nail Broth"); *Southwest Review* ("Eulogy for an Anchorite"); *TriQuarterly* ("Nettles of the Field"); *Virginia Quarterly Review* ("Falcon Channel," "Wallenda Sutra," "Zoopraxiscope Sutra"). "A Colonial Epitaph Annotated" was reprinted in the sixth edition of *The Compact Bedford Introduction to Literature*, edited by Michael Meyer (Boston: Bedford/St. Martin's, 2003). Grateful thanks are extended also to the Yaddo Colony and the St. Botolph Club for their vital support.

WONDER ✷ CABINET

. . . a goodly huge cabinet, wherein whatsoever the hand
of man by exquisite art or engine hath made rare in stuff,
form, or motion; whatsoever singularity, chance, and the shuffle
of things hath produced; whatsoever Nature hath wrought in things
that want life and may be kept; shall be sorted and included.
Francis Bacon

PILGRIM'S PROGRESS

The fin is the finest thing of its kind.
The wing's a wonder the world over.
The tongue is a form of eternal flame.
The stone's a story that never grows old.

O fin, it's certain you want for nothing.
Yo wing, you're everything we've ever dreamed.
You said it, tongue: of arms and men you sing.
Here's looking at you, stone: a star is born.

Who doesn't burn for a soul on the wing?
Where is the man that can fine-tune the fin?
When shall we learn to read the mind of the stone?
What in the world holds its own like the tongue?

Stone says fin's the one that schooled the wing.
Story goes one singer could charm the stones.
Rock, paper, scissors: worlds without end.
One slip of the tongue makes the whole world kin.

All together now: the many in the one.
Brush fire of fins shirring the fathoms,
Cairns of lost tongues, the chorus in the wings
Riffing on the omens of the heavens.

Soul knows it can't live on breath alone.
When the tongue wags the dog, the fur's gonna fly.
The stone is a kind of recording angel.
The wing's got the beat. The fin makes waves.

Wing it, mother tongue: the world's your whetstone.
We're wired for sound. We're unfinished business.
Let's hear it for the phoenix, all fired up.
Sirens, rock us to sleep with the fishes.

Let's hear it for descent with variations.
Let him without fin go back to the grindstone.
The bat is the manta ray's soul brother.
The dolphin's glossolalia speaks volumes.

Hosannas for sea changes, the wish made flesh.
As the silkworm turns, as the chrysalis
Is my witness, leviathan's no fluke.
Blood from a stone is a thing to behold.

Blow me down with a feather, fishers of men;
Rock of ages, take me under your wing.
Muse, make it new: leave no tongue untuned.
Rock my world, winged gods: begin again.

CALENTURE

Then as the possessed with Calentura thou shalt offer to leape.
Thomas Nashe

When the briny slop turned woody and sweet,
You'd be clapped in irons belowdecks.
And there were other classic signs:
Sheaves in the combers, floating pastures,
Parish meadows hard to starboard.

Heatstroke, heartsick—it didn't matter.
The peril was real. Yonder were green fields.
The murmuring glade, the beckoning hollow,
Hovered there in the glassy swell.
If you weren't restrained, you'd leap headlong.

When the fever broke, you saw things plain.
Oh, rub your poor skull like a scoured shell,
Pray you're one tar who's cured for good.
Yet there you were still: thin reed, short fuse,
And glare on a wave, breaking into leaf.

CHIMERICAL

Cook's men couldn't conjure
A moniker for the creature.
Whilst the *Endeavour* lay aground
There in the longitude
Of upside down (spring
No spring, but more like fall),
They bandied and brainstormed,
Thunderstruck. The shrunken forelimbs
Stumped all hands—tucked up
On the chest as if saying grace
Or a misfit manacled
In the brig.
        But what a clip!
Hopscotched upright, fleet
As a deer (great clouds in the bush,
Catapulting off, spooked),
Long tail scrolled
Like a lord's greyhound,
Though in carriage akin
To a titan hare.
        Bagged one,
Skinned it (secret pocket,
Like a turncoat's), pondered long
The daunting haunch, but the sum
Of the parts still tied them
In knots.
        O abounding conundrum,
Where's your Adam?
By what rough magic
Does a rubric stick?

Hop to it, mates—
Every lingua franca takes
A leap of faith.
Here's one for the books,
A real kicker:
The woolly Calibans
Who roamed those hinterlands
Bamboozled the ship's naturalists
But good, the cognomen
Now known the world round
Signifying *I don't know*
In the local singsong.

A kind of rune, then,
A koan that rules (Can a ruse
Ring true? Why rue the day?),
Be it tongue in cheek
Or a rumor with legs,
A con all along
Or the old switcheroo:
Cantankerous, inscrutable,
A congeries in any lexicon,
Uncanny through and through,
A cantilevered ruminant,
A kangaroo.

A COLONIAL EPITAPH ANNOTATED

HERE LIES AS SILENT CLAY
MISS ARABELLA YOUNG
WHO ON THE 21ST OF MAY 1771
BEGAN TO HOLD HER TONGUE.

Here rests as circumspect dust
A maid who spoke her mind
Without the ghost of a blush
Or a nod to her prim kind.

Here silt her tart remarks
And her spirited retorts,
Her mordant takes on politics
And the sermon's finer points.

Here chafes in stony hush
An erstwhile spitfire.
Finally they could rest in peace,
The fools she wouldn't suffer!

Here in her boneyard bower
Look sharp for the shards of a quip.
The lady was no flower.
She'd cut you to the quick.

Here beneath this slate
You can sense her mute dismay,
Who was the soul of wit
And reveled in repartee.

Here lies as silent clay
Miss Arabella Young.
Be that as it may,
Here's to the sting in her tongue.

EULOGY FOR AN ANCHORITE

Brother Adam, devout bee breeder,
Today the paper ran your obit.
A brisk write-up, yet how it brims
With the lambent amber of your bliss.
Your abiding faith in the honeybee
Imbued your days with abounding grace.

"Brother Adam, Benedictine monk,
Transformed beekeeping, at 98 . . ."
I adore that squib. I laud your slant
On beatitude and humble soulcraft.
I love the fact your name was gold
In apiaries around the globe.

Brother Adam, from Buckfast Abbey
In Britain's toe, you would abscond
(Often on foot or astride a donkey)
To Araby and the Holy Land,
There to bushwhack for robust strains
To husband in your cloistered hives.

At ninety, admirable Brother Adam,
You bobbed to the top of Kilimanjaro
Strapped to the back of a kindred spirit
In pursuit of the burly Monticola.
Brother Adam, that took some aplomb.
It buoys me simply to think of it.

O Brother Adam, if I may be so bold,
You must have harbored no higher rapture
Than when a swarm's harmonious hubbub
Swelled into a thrumming rumble.
The heather bloomed, the nectar flowed:
What choir ever soared any sweeter?

You're the stuff of fable, Brother Adam.
Your little sisters, how they labor!
We sybarites owe you a lasting debt.
To spurn the temptations of the flesh
Only to leave the world more toothsome—
Now, there's a parable to savor.

Brother Adam, redoubtable beekeeper,
You belong on the glazed pane of a chapel
Bedecked in your habit and your veil
Hard by the other miracle workers.
There hovers about you a burnished aura
Befitting a harbinger of ambrosia.

Brother Adam, Brother Adam,
When it comes to combs, you split the atom.
Every kingdom has its keys.
They've baptized your hybrids "superbees."
The heartbreaking millennium runs down,
But, Brother Adam, your renown's a balm.

Brother Adam, I'm no believer.
When I'm not bedeviled, I'm beleaguered.
But consider your bees, in clover season—
Didn't they seem possessed by demons?
Let me grapple, let me fumble.
I may yet become your true disciple.

SHADES OF ALEXANDRIA

Cosmologists, epic poets, holy men in exile—
They all found their way to the illustrious library.
All lovers of knowledge were welcome to a niche
In that bristling hush, no matter how shaggy or ragged.

There were the usual cynics and the inevitable stoics.
Some were sages without honor, scrawling out summas
In their mongrel dialects and inscrutable cuneiforms,
Working those little golf pencils right down to the nub.

There were the astronomers, who stayed up every night
Observing the movements of the firmament:
You could tell by their bloodshot stares and rumpled garb
How resolutely they pursued their lucubrations.

Some looked as if they'd studied under Aristotle—
Ancient souls, tottering about like crusty Nile tortoises,
Griping over the plague of errors infesting the card catalogues.
You'd hear them mutter darkly as they tussled with the drawers.

Sophists, peripatetics, soothsayers, tragedians—
None were turned away, you didn't question
This one's erudition or that one's chosen discipline.
The collections were open to scribes of every persuasion.

From the ends of the earth the seekers would come
Just to incline their heads over our long tables.
And if they slumped forward altogether on occasion,
Who could possibly object—the dream of reason

Is like unto the fathomless siftings of the sands,
Everlasting study is a weariness of the flesh.
You could tell by their soiled bundles and open sores
How profoundly they suffered for their great life's work.

One would think that there in the vaulted reading room
You could count on a modicum of classical decorum,
But you know how scholars are, jealous of their turf,
Forever denouncing their rivals as barbarians.

And to tell the truth, few of them were distinguished—
Whatever acumen they once may have possessed
They'd squandered on pedantry of dubious import.
Most seemed to be glossing corruptions in the texts.

And if you were a page—that's what we were known as then,
Back when the world was young—you picked up after them,
You reshelved the strewn compendiums and lexicons,
You inspected the rune-scored stalls at closing time

To make sure there were no thinkers lost in contemplation.
Satirists, orators, votaries of Ptolemy and Diogenes—
You'd shepherd them out the swinging double doors
Into the misty or sticky evening, the bay's salt bite,

The streets with their attar of dumpster and flask.
One day was like another in that seat of learning.
Creeping hours, turning leaves, cracked spines, and paper cuts—
Here you spoke in whispers, and history held its breath.

INQUEST

Edward Andrews, put to the crank
For pinching four pounds of English beef,
Couldn't keep up the wicked pace.
He wrecked the thing, as a matter of fact.

The prison committee reviewed his case.
What had gone wrong with the machine?
Edward Andrews, a lad of fifteen,
Had somehow managed to botch the works.

Birmingham Gaol believed in reform.
The iron drum was filled with sand.
The crank turned an axle, mounted with scoops,
And the dial clicked off an accurate count.

Ten thousand revolutions a day—
Grinding away, yet milling nothing.
Ten thousand revolutions a day?
How had they come by that round number?

There was a science to the sentence.
Hard labor, the lever of correction,
Demanded standard units of measure.
According to their calculations,

The reprobate's required exertions
Worked out to a quarter of the force
An English draft horse was known to muster
Over an equivalent span of hours.

Bridle, did he, our Edward Andrews?
Hard to figure. On three occasions
He went at the crank, and thrice he failed
To dispatch his per diem.

On the third go-round, the dial jammed.
So there was nothing for it then
But to make young Andrews rue his ways
By binding up his feeble arms.

Routine practice: the "punishment jacket,"
All of leather, pinched tight at the neck.
Hours at a stretch, a parching throat
Awaited the miscreant who spit the bit.

Naturally questions had to be asked
Once Edward Andrews was laid to rest.
(He'd hanged himself by his hammock strap.)
Open and shut: not even a right brute,

Much less a boy, all skin and bones,
Could summon up the staying power
To churn the dune inside the drum
On prison rations, bread and water.

There is no turning back the clock.
The desperate are always with us.
Here's Edward Andrews, still at the crank.
Watch him go: a ghost in the flesh.

THUMBNAIL SKETCH OF THE TULIPMANIA

At the peak of a fever like none other,
A good burgher whose thrift was his repute
Might part with two hogsheads of vintage port,
Twelve stout ewes and eight fat swine,
A silver chalice and a suit of clothes,
And brick after wheel after brick of cheese
For a single bulb and fancy himself shrewd.
The logs disclose another who swapped a mill,
And one a brewery, for their fabled specimens.

Clouds of golden pollen. The pages crackle.
All Holland's in thrall—the tulips have souls.

Cultivated by sultans, "turbans" from the Persians,
Imported for the delectation of the courts
And the jaded palates of the capitals:
Laced with oil and vinegar in London
And in Dresden powdered with sugar.
But the Dutchman's taste ran to *tulpenwoede*—
Florid euphoria, epidemic ardor.
In the smoky taverns of Haarlem and Utrecht,
Flame-tongued goblets fed a blaze of speculation.

A fever like none other. The pages smolder.
The souls of tulips are mulched with Holland's gold.

Before the bottom fell out, before the bubble burst,
There were fortunes to be made from the mutations
That engendered hybrids by the hundredfold.
Pleats and ruffles, scarlet wicks and creamy swatches,

The ruby-veined undercup of the Semper Augustus,
From tightfisted roots the treasured clusters breaking open—
Behold the veritable bounty of beauty!
In vain the preachers thundered from their pulpits.
When obsession's in bloom, it beggars all reason.

The tulips had souls—all Holland said so.
A spiked dust flares above the gilded pages.

MASTERS OF THE FLORILEGIUM

You copied out passages as the spirit moved you.
You took down verses to cultivate rapture.
Lessons of the fathers, lives of the saints,
Hallowed utterances—these were your cuttings,
Your verdant devotions and fertile verities.

Lectionis igne—"fervent reading."
Candle-tremble and cramped longhand.
Leaves of scripture, tendrils of parable.
You bound your gleanings into vellum booklets.
You wet a fingertip and found your place.

Little anthologies, anonymous garlands.
Florilegium—"from flower to flower."
And from your cells, a steady murmuring:
Tongues working, text and script
Like nectar on your moving lips.

It was understood you could intermingle
Spontaneous lines, original images.
For there on the page—*sacra pagina*—
Transcription begets inspiration.
What you parse becomes a part of you.

"He who is possessed by the sweetness of prayer,"
Wrote John the Grammarian, "already participates
In heavenly life." And Peter the Venerable,
Upon a brother's passing, heard to cry: "Without resting,
His mouth ruminated the sacred words."

FROM A BURBANK CATALOGUE

Luther Burbank, *New Creations in Fruits and Flowers* (1893)

I. "A THORNLESS CACTUS"

Everything he touches is a work in progress.
Give him another good six or seven years
And he will bring you a generous slab of cactus

Marred only by a few indifferent nubs.
Give him another ten and he will deliver
A specimen as blameless as a newborn's cheek.

Already he can take them in his hands.
And in time they'll be unable even to leave
These feeble scratches—or should he say unwilling?

From the window he watches the first light
Tint their clusters pink; he watches their cusps
Glaze scarlet as the sun goes down.

Graft by graft, he is mending the ways
Of the fallen world, its perils and its errors,
Leaving less and less cause for bristling rancor

Or reason to quarrel with flesh and blood.
Give him the lion's share of a lifetime
And he will show you how covert solicitude

Can coax away all memory of earthly harm,
Every trace of mistrust, each ingrained wish
To slash inquisitive fingertips.

As if to affirm for us that sweetness
Knows no natural limits, as if to attest

To a destiny where infinite possibility
Will be the true and only gospel of the land.

As if to bequeath us the blueprints
By which we might fashion profusion.

As if the various shades of ink and blood
Gave rise to an orchard of cloven vowels.

As if the twilight skies reprise their skin.
As if their flesh were understudying the moon.

Purple Flame, Abundance, Elephant Heart,
Climax, Red Ace, Apex, Epoch . . .

And best of all the nameless harvests
Yet to come, with their adamant promises

Of an earlier blossoming and later ripening,
A braver tang, a freer stone, a finer luster—

As if to see himself as the appointed amanuensis
Called upon to take a lavish dictation

In a lost tongue, as if to hand down a volume
Composed entirely of premonitions and inflections.

III. "HANDKERCHIEFS ON THE LAWN"

Famous for its diffidence, the evening primrose waits
For light to fail before unclasping. But the ones
He has arrayed in perfect schoolroom rows

Between the plot of gladioli and the verbena beds
Are learning the virtues of opening
With alacrity, extending the span of their blossoms

Beyond their wildest intentions. No longer
Can they be coveted for their pale hands
Cupped to receive an even share of mild chill:

He has bred in them an urgency and willfulness,
A flair for wanderlust. And so by now
He can no longer say they greet him

As he returns from the greenhouse at dusk—
Each hand now grasps a rippling handkerchief
In the customary manner of farewells.

He would like to think they are leaving behind
The cant of a crabbed and fearful world,
A shipload of sturdy pilgrims setting forth

On the strength of his luminous convictions.
He would like to think they are waving goodbye
To the bedrock of luck and accident.

APHRODITE'S MOUSETRAP

When did the literal ever stay put?
Old John Bartram had a pet name for it,
The cunning little plant with a lust
For flesh. It tickled the King's Botanist

To shock his guests with his "tipitiwitchet"—
Letting it work its touchy witchery,
Watching them flinch. Innocent it wasn't:
Spring-trap leaves, all red inside, sticky wickets

Fringed with bristles, wickedly snapping shut
On any prey that fell into its clutches.
Everything about it was explicit,
But specimens need names, and the fantastic

Has to have its say. Call it what you like,
A fig leaf it's not. For many a wit
Of a rakish bent, Bartram's dirty joke
Might as well have been spelled out in scarlet:

A collar made of fur was called a "tippet"—
Hence the "hempen tippet," wastrel argot
For the hangman's noose—and with a bent stick
And a trip wire, you could rig a "twitch-up"

For snaring rabbits and other small pelts,
Which is the tip-off for what was meant
By "twitchet," once a common epithet
In vulgar parlance for that privy part

Which legend had it was built to snatch
One's member like a maw, complete with teeth.
What man could help but squirm at the sight?
Here was a wildflower utterly unladylike,

Wanton, treacherous, lying in wait.
No nonsense, Bartram's waggish sobriquet
Clinches it with a titillating flourish,
Though now it sounds like so much gibberish,

Which is why for a while it was thought
He'd picked up the name from a medicine man
In the Carolinas, from whence it sprang.
Hard to say how many ears pricked up

At the time, but lest there be a wisp of doubt
That certain learned gentlemen got the gist,
Consult your field guide. To be exact,
There's no tiptoeing past those racy italics:

Dionaea muscipula, a knowing wink
In the newfangled binomial dialect.
Parse it as you wish, it's rated X—
The classical goddess of all things erotic

Was the offspring of the titaness Dione,
With whom her myth was ofttimes confounded,
And properly speaking, the predicate
Can only be Englished as "mousetrap,"

And there you have it, Bartram's whatchamacallit
Laid bare beyond all semantic dispute.
Who's to say what's patently indecent?
Taxonomy's not for the delicate:

Long live the King's English, but by Venus,
Let no schoolmarm besmirch our mother wit.
One man's anathema is another man's tonic,
And woman's too, for all that divides us.

BALLADE OF THE GOLDEN ARM

GOD OF BIRDS, BUT SCOURGE OF FOXES AND BADGERS
newspaper headline

Dateline Bokonbayeva, Kyrgyzstan:
"He loves me, and he knows that I love him."
Meet the old *berkutchi* master: one Sulayman-
Bekov Kutuldu, golden eagle on his arm.
Hunting season's nearly here, time soon to comb
Their sawtooth realm for game. And how tenderly
He murmurs, stroking his longtime companion:
"We understand each other perfectly."

Only in Kyrgyzstan and next-door Kazakhstan
Can such eagle men be found. In fighting trim,
A blood-sport dream team, Merlin with a griffon.
The *berkutchi* is the keeper of this flame:
Lightning on the wing, the original smart bomb.
Let the young turks trifle with falconry!
Mark his words: "Other voices mean nothing to him.
We understand each other perfectly."

Slugline Kyrgyzstan, east of no-man's-land,
Halfway to the moon. Here still the ancient custom
Survives as if by the decree of a grand khan.
Hood a brawny nestling, crooning as it screams,
Then for three days straight induce acute delirium—
No scraps, no sleep. The rest is alchemy:
Two iron wills, one golden mean, and in good time
They understand each other perfectly.

Stop the presses! The gauntlet's been thrown down.
What's love if not this call to arms, this perfect fury?
Come what promised land or peaceable kingdom
Will we understand each other this perfectly?

FALCON CHANNEL

It's coming to you live: the high-rise ledge
That doubles as a desolate precipice
In a pinch. It's all raw footage,

Cutting-edge surveillance, one tight shot
Trained on the cornice of a downtown complex
Handpicked for its head-spinning drop

And instant access to whistling updrafts.
Soap opera, talk-show catfight, floor of Congress,
Fleecing infomercial, play-off highlights,

And now this: heroic measures, last-gasp habitat,
A breeding pair banded and released
Atop a glass spire in the scudding firmament.

It carries no viewer-discretion notice,
So be advised: the content can be graphic,
Their taste for gore may give you gooseflesh,

And you may fairly quail at that ticked-off look
They always wear, no matter what,
Like the dapper heavies in a cult mob flick.

The winds that whip past their bitter parapet
Would make your eyes tear if you were there,
But this way, whenever you feel up to it,

You can surf the ether to the lip of their roost
And snoop at will while they gorge and preen
As if you were a spirit or a hard-boiled spook.

It's come to pass: things fall apart.
This makeshift bluff is their last best haunt.
It's a breaking story, time is short,

It's not for the squeamish or the faint of heart.
There may be a dull ache in your wrist
As you punch them up on your remote,

There may be moments when you wish
You could program the minicam to blink.
This just in: it's come to this.

SOURCE

On the eloquence of the Indians of that land,
Fray Antonio is still the one to read.
Wool of various colors, raveled into strands,

Each strand consisting of finely knotted threads
And about as thick as a rope or iron spindle.
By the color they knew the meaning of each thread:

Yellow stood for gold, white for silver, red for soldiers.
Fray Antonio finds this precision admirable.
Such things as had no color were placed by order

In keeping with what was counted as most noble.
Hence when tallying the arms of their legions
(Fray Antonio bristles with instructive examples),

First lances, then javelins, clubs, and so on,
A knot for each and every sling and arrow.
And so too for the souls of their dominions:

A knot for every tenth elder, vassal, warrior,
By province and by station, in like fashion—
And woe to the weaver who let slip an error!

Fray Antonio proceeds by demonstration.
He wants his reader to grasp the intricacy
Of the system and its boundless applications

For that vast unlettered empire's ruling hierarchy:
Not merely were these skeins their running ledgers,
Inventories of the most exacting accuracy,

But their annals, archives, and chronicles,
The veritable fabric of their history and their destiny,
Their laws and prophecies and holy scriptures.

All this naturally demanded the utmost mastery
And constant study. On that caste of sworn adepts,
The *Quipo Camayos,* those appointed secretaries

Whose office it was to learn by heart the knots,
Fray Antonio is nothing if not cogent.
Never could they permit their memory to lapse

When parsing what the strands and threads all meant,
For if one of their number *deviated a hair's breadth*
From the truth, or gave a contradictory account

Of an event, he would be swiftly put to death.
Each therefore stuck to his own special field
So that none would ever be out of his depth

In any telling detail and all would be revealed
In accordance with the edicts of the overlord.
And in this manner they recorded how their world

Came to be: arrayed against a black cord,
Signifying time, threads the color of straw
And knots by the thousands—then, like a word

From above, a great knot spliced with an awe-
Inspiring band of finespun sovereign crimson,
For here began the royal line and rule of law

And here commenced the annual festival of the sun
(A spidery knot for every ritual sacrifice)
And here a revolt was quashed and here the scion

Of the tyrant (the knots denote the time and place)
Fasted on a precipice until the god of the sea foam
Spoke unto him and ushered in an age of peace.

Although Fray Antonio does not presume
To translate at length from the Inca canon,
His investigations have more than persuaded him

That nothing exceeded their powers of expression.
For as it was knotted, so was it written—
Fact by taut fact, or by sinuous allusion.

Thus by omission they understood what had not been.
Before there were kings these people were barbarians.
Some of the threads had other fine threads wound in . . .

For the plain colors and the mixed ones
All had their own meanings. And let it be noted
That some have been found in the form of confessions,

And some were meant to be sung like a ballad,
And some were omens, which no man could dissemble.
Not for a moment can their fluency be doubted,

But sooner lash a llama through the eye of a needle
Than ask whereby they acquired this skill
Or how their fingers got to be so nimble.

His sources contend that they do not excel
Any longer at this art, but on that thought
Fray Antonio does not see fit to dwell:

Have not the holy the world over always taught
That however prolific or dexterous,
Man's handiwork cannot but come to naught?

All that notwithstanding, there's nothing censorious
In Fray Antonio's tone; on the contrary,
No passage could lavish more praise on their prowess.

Fray Antonio is compiling the official history
Of Peru's Augustine order, but such are the wonders
And the marvels of this his native country

(Born in 1584, in a cloud-high mining center)
He doesn't always stick to his knitting.
Never did anyone hear a clap of thunder

There, he avows elsewhere, *or see a ray of lightning.*

SYMPATHY FOR THE MAPINGUARI

Dear monster, I fear you're no longer in demand.
The folklore's in dispute, the annals a tangle.
We're supposed to write you off as spurious,
But I'm not one to leave well enough alone.

The folklore's in dispute, an arrant tangle
Of wanton conjecture and embroidered hunches.
Nonetheless, I can't leave well enough alone:
The beast in us knows a soul mate when it sees one.

A welter of conjecture, patchwork hunches—
Yeti-like, yet hewing to the steaming jungle.
The beast in us knows a soul mate when it seizes one:
Tracks in the muck, "like people's, only backwards."

Yeti-like, yet hewing to the steeping Amazon,
You have ways of making your presence known.
Your murky tracks ("like people's, only backwards")
Point straight to the canopy's eternal glooms.

You have ways of making your presence known.
Sometimes you bellow. Sometimes you hoot or weep.
Pointing stiffly at a curtain of infernal gloom,
A rancher vouches that you croon there half the night.

Sometimes you bellow. Sometimes you whimper.
And on occasion you'll ambush an innocent.
A rubber tapper swears you lunged at him one night:
Half mooncalf, half ape, a gruesome blur of flesh.

On occasion you'll ambush a penitent.
It's essential to keep up appearances.
A full-blown missing link, fearsomeness incarnate—
And still one hears those slurs that you're a figment!

It's imperative to keep up appearances,
But I suspect your heart just isn't in it.
You've heard the ugly slurs. An utter figment!
That's a black mark no bête noire can live down.

Why do I sense your heart's no longer in it?
Call it instinct; or else a phantom pain.
There are bum raps no abomination can abide
As long as skin can crawl and blood runs cold.

Call it instinct, perhaps a fateful pang—
I refuse to brush you off as dubious.
So long as there is marrow in these bones,
Fear not, dark familiar: you're still the man.

ODE TO WILLIAM WELLS

William Wells, this is to tell you that the morning wet
Still beads the leaves with precision and abandon.
Comes now your beloved creeping damp, even as I write.

What possessed you, William Wells, what iridescent hypothesis
Sent you out like a serial phantom into London's clammy lanes?
What gists did you distill from the droplet's hieroglyphics?

Doctor, your undertaking absorbs me when I'm up late.
There's a touch of the sublime in your arcane fixation.
I can almost picture you eyeballing pearly spider's lace . . .

But alas, posterity wipes the slate. Your "Essay on Dew,"
Admired in its day, has gone the way of all condensation.
You're a footnote if you're lucky: foreshadower of Darwin,

Royal Society regular, expatriate physician from the States
With a bent for natural philosophy, a minor evolutionist.
Your proofs are lost on us. Your opus molders in the stacks.

And how on earth could it be otherwise? Your chosen field
Was any garden margin at its peak of superficial glister.
Your realm of inquiry could only prove demonstrably ephemeral.

William Wells, you are obscure—you've turned to mist.
So humor my surmises in these small hours. Hear me out:
Each grass spear in my side yard bears your watermark;

The morning glories I'm letting have their way this year
Batten the pickets in soaking tangles, a diorama in your honor.
Everywhere I look the undergrowth jewels up and there you are.

William Wells, transpire what may before I'm dust,
Let me take a leaf from you: ardent and intent
On noting well what burns away, what cannot last.

NEW WORLD SUTRAS

HOUDINI SUTRA

The small box is filled
With me and air; the large box
Is filled with water.

Let air have its fill
Of me. When I free myself,
Water never tells.

Inside there's a roar,
But I'm playing it by ear,
Cool as a river.

Big hand for the man
Who can think outside the box
Little by little.

Escape hinges on
My wherewithal. Go fathom.
After me, the flood.

The small box is locked
Inside the large box. Water
Seeks its own devil.

He who is artful
Washes his hands of the odds,
Wishful no longer.

File me under
Up in the air. Pour me out
Like a waterfall.

Small world, all full
Of dear old air. Everywhere
I flow, there I am.

Submerge me. Write my
Name in water. Give a wave
When there's no me there.

WALLENDA SUTRA

Life's on the wire;
The rest is waiting. I know
I'm alive when I

Hear no one breathing.
On the wire I'm living:
The wire is where

I'm sure where I stand
In the great chain of being.
The rest is dead air;

The rest is waiting.
When I'm out on the wire,
Beyond all wanting,

It's clear that the rest
Of my life is sleepwalking.
Stadiums, gorges,

Standing room only—
That's me in the viewfinder,
Making my living.

Life's on the wire,
Where everything's trembling;
The rest is nothing

But worry and care.
On the wire I'm at one
With all my past lives,

Treading the fine line
Between the worms and the stars.
The rest is stalling;

The rest is chafing.
Wherever there's wires, that's
Where I'll be waiting.

GREAT STONE FACE SUTRA

Let the blank slate be
The essence of your silence.
Be the one who moves

In sync with mayhem,
Rebuffing your undoing
In fluent deadpan.

If all else fails,
Take a tumble, bust a move,
Let your mind reel.

When your luck runs out,
Dash after it, one hand clamped
On your porkpie hat.

Be the one who falls
Flawlessly, keeping your cool
At a breakneck clip,

Licking fixes catch
As catch can, dumb like a sphinx,
Not once cracking up.

Loose lips seal flops.
Be the one for whom double
Takes do the talking.

On cue, be a blur.
Conjure a gadget. Never
Let them see you smart.

Let the cyclone howl,
Let bridges burn to cinders,
Let cats have your tongue—

You'll still be the one
Who goes for broke in the dark
For your dying art.

IGNATZ SUTRA

Call me krazy. Keep
Me dizzy. Show no mercy,
My L'il Ainjil.

Will care kill a puss?
No dice, pet. Call me loco,
Knock me off my feet.

Konk me kooky. Drive
Me batty. Don't be sorry:
You can skin this kat

Any way you like.
By the crook in my tail
I shall plight my troth.

Zip—Zap—Pow! Ka-bomp!
Make me see stars, rain your bricks
Down on my noggin,

Kit and kaboodle:
I only have google eyes
For you, my inkling.

Call me cuckoo. Clock
Me, plunk me, willy-nilly:
I go all woozy

When I get lucky.
Pucker up, my paper wasp.
I'm dumbstruck for keeps.

Ring my trolley. Slap
Me happy, every Sunday:
Our strip of wasteland

Is my nirvana.
Call it a krazy kwilt. Call
It Amerika.

Who needs the claptrap
In the fishwrap? I'll kowtow
Till the clouds come home

To roost, my pindrop.
Valentine, there's no vaccine
For what flails me.

Call me loony. Bonk
Me only. Brain me, crown me
In all your glory.

SATCHMO SUTRA

What we play is life.
What we play with is fire.
The beat is the spark,

Hotter than ever.
Swing, You Cats. Sugar Foot Stomp.
What we vamp is mint,

What we blast is sweet.
When we're grooving, we're golden,
Thunder and lightning:

Hot Five, Hot Seven,
This here's fire we're stealing.
Play it like whiplash,

Play it on the spot.
Tight Like This. Hotter Than That.
When we're swinging, we're

Winging it, blazing
The way: unheard-of uproar
Is the new frontier,

Faster than ever
But never in a hurry.
What we dig is din,

What we blow turns blue.
Muskrat Ramble. Tiger Rag.
We play it by ear

With mojo to burn.
Gabriel's got nothing on
This horn of plenty,

This golden blossom
Redeems pandemonium.
Darktown to Dreamland,

We blow the house down.
Shanghai Shuffle. Georgia Grind.
Let there be nightlife,

Fireworks in key:
This here stop-time's a cakewalk,
Bah-de-do-da-day.

What we play is life.
We were born to breathe fire.
The beat is our torch:

You can't touch our chops.
O volcano reveille,
Glorious ruckus—

Worlds collide when
We riff something fierce. Our work
Is to play in the

Heat of the moment.
What we're playing is changing
Life as we know it.

BAMBINO SUTRA

Swing with everything
You've got. Sock it and admire
The arc. This is what

The game is about.
This is the house my clouts built.
Here comes another

Mammoth rip, here comes
My patented thunderclap.
This is the way to

Make the old game grand
Again, going deep in the
Packed house my clouts built.

Here comes Colossus,
Batting cleanup. There goes a
Moon shot, upper deck.

This is the power
They write home about. This is
The house my clouts built.

Swing for the fences,
Bunyanesque. Everyone loves
A majestic blast

That defies the laws
Of matter and space, the stuff
That myths are made of.

This is the sweet spot
That runs with the grain, the snap
In the wrists that makes

The old lumber ring,
The leonine reflexes
In an ursine frame

That packs the punch that
Wins the crown for the home team
That's built around me.

Swing as if this swing
Will be your last. Even my
Whiffs are feats of strength.

This is the press box,
Where the scribes wax Homeric,
This is the bull pen,

Where the aces sweat
Bullets. This is my playhouse:
My wallops built it.

Where is it written
You have to grow up? Make way
For the man-child,

All brawn and pinstripes,
That mugs for the shutterbugs
That feast on the swats

That put the fannies
In the seats. Ladies and gents,
Hold on to your hats—

This is my sandbox,
My ballyard, my turf. This is
The house my clouts built.

DOUBLE ELEPHANT FOLIO SUTRA

Great works make great leaps.
All the birds shall have a place.
All shall be like life.

Great sheets for the plates,
All the greatness of likeness
Now coming to light

Like never on earth.
All are in their element.
None shall be left out.

All the plumes must gleam,
All the eyes must be embers,
All must be captured

In living color,
True to scale, flourishing
In their native haunts.

Great is the least tern
And the little green heron.
All hail the lark,

Who summons the sun;
Bow down to the great horned owl,
Our lord of the gloom.

Great sheets for the sky,
The sea swell and the summits,
The vanishing point

Beyond the great plains.
All shall be as planned, not a
Feather out of place.

All must be hunting,
Courting, swooping, quarreling,
Brandishing their wings

Like fans or long knives.
Great pains with the tints and inks:
Rubythroat, goldfinch,

Indigo bunting,
Gyrfalcon in both phases,
Black death and ghost dance.

Our great age of prints
Demands no less: here is where
The great auk shall plash

To its heart's content
And the only paroquet
In our hemisphere

Still revel in all
Its brilliance, brash as new bills,
A flying circus.

All shall be complete.
It must be a work of art.
Some will swear they hear

Gulls mewling, bitterns
Booming, drumming woodpeckers,
Ravens swapping quips.

Great works take great leaps
Of faith. None shall be left out.
All shall be like life.

ZOOPRAXISCOPE SUTRA

Bodies in motion
Leave us lasting impressions.
Ghosts of an instant

Spring into action.
One thoroughbred's stride is a
Feast for the senses:

This wheel of life
Makes all motion momentous.
Negatives don't lie,

You are not dreaming—
The persistence of vision
Is no illusion.

Faster is truer.
Swift comes the answer: stills in
Succession shall make

Sense of commotion.
Dark horse on the loose, out of
Reason and Passion,

Teach us the secrets
Of your molten momentum,
Stealing a march on

Blind speculation.
Seconds shall be split into
Breathtaking fractions—

Motion no longer
A maelstrom, a miasma.
The future is now,

Flowing in focus:
This wheel of life makes all
Action auspicious.

Seize the daylight. Shoot
The works. Capture creation.
This is no time to

Ration compulsion.
One colt's cloud of dust is an
Epic explosion.

Faster is truer.
Now we're all seers. Out of
The whirlwind comes

Sweeping revision,
A procession of phantoms.
No magic lantern

Can hold a candle
To this running series of
Lightning exposures:

Blazing forms frozen,
Then spun back into motion.
Later is sooner,

Horses are wishes.
This wheel of life makes all
Vision voracious.

Motion has spoken.
You are not delirious.
Action breeds vision,

Shadows complete us.
This wheel of life turns all
Of us luminous.

LULLABY IN STEERAGE

Bright globes you'll pluck with a twist,
My sweet. Keep still while you can.
Stars on your kitchen tiles,
Birds that come to your hand.
Streets like shipping lanes,
Gosling: many will be yours.
Save your breath for the bandstand
Sing-alongs, save those tears
For the moving picture shows.
Roses threading the trellis,
Dearest, roses under your cheek
As you sink into pillow feathers,
Pearls cool on your throat.
By then your hair will be white,
My lamb. By then you won't believe
That you were ever a howling babe
Delivered up out of the sea.
By then we'll just be a story
You'll hear as you're drifting off
In your sky-blue room on visiting day,
So hush now, precious, hush.
Listen to them make us up
And tuck you into my shawl.
Listen, child, the channel buoys
Are church bells after all.

TAR PIT

If you've ever seen one bubble up, you don't forget.
Reeking pitch, glossy sludge in heaving gouts,
Steeping muck that devours and preserves.

If in the presence of all that brooding pressure
You were instructed to imagine the untold volumes,
You can't stop now, you still can't help but shiver.

Patient chemical ferment, opulent and desolate.
If your eyes played over it, you saw stained glass.
If you clutched the cyclone fence, your feet would squinch.

And didn't it give off a stench like everyone's garage?
And weren't you the one who dreamed your own backyard
Began to ooze sweet crude from a hidden seam?

Once you have learned it could suck a mammoth down,
Why not a home? Why not a whole sheltered childhood
Sealed away from all that flenses and bleaches?

Animal and mineral, the mother of all mires.
Why turn away now? Why, you were born near there,
No more than a dire wolf's howl away. You know full well

There's not a fen can touch it when it comes
To what's forbidden, nor a bog on God's green earth
So firm with bone and all that's bred therein.

What is there to fear? There is so much there,
If it came in drums it would last you a lifetime.
Dream on, go ahead, stick that broad brush right in:

You can make your own rank slick that simmers and stews,
You can slather it on in rich heaping glops
So that nothing escapes, not a grief, not one hurt.

If you loved how it fumed and seethed, how can you deny
It smacks of every livid urge that's in your blood?
If all the world were a glade, what would you have to forgive?

FUNICULAR

Funny word, all full of itself. Could be some old joke:
A guttersnipe's malaprop for a private part
Or Caesar's babble on *Your Show of Shows,* winging a rant.

Here it comes now: rattle and clank down the bare sharp bluff
And then back up, going nowhere not so fast.
You're rising or sinking, that's how the physics works—

Each car functions as the other's counterweight,
One turtling downslope, one trundling skyward.
Grinding by, they nearly touch. Funny thing,

A shell of itself, a little rail trip back in time.
Same old story: swank hotels and Queen Anne mansions
On the heights, the market district honeycombed below.

From *funiculus:* a rope or line worked by a cable or the like.
Also, in anatomy, a conducting cord such as a nerve cord
Or the umbilical. Once a nickel took you from one world

To the other in a snap—a minute each way, chop-chop,
But saving you from a hellacious flight of steps.
"World's Shortest Railway"—that must have had a funny ring

Even in 1901, for after all this was old Los Angeles,
Up and coming, the city the Southern Pacific built.
And here's the punch line: they dubbed it Angels Flight,

Playing all the angles to the hilt. Get this:
The first compartments looked like open baskets
But were soon replaced by the classic trolley cars,

Which were then christened after those hallowed summits
In the Holy Land, Sinai and Olivet. Round and round
They chuffed, sunup to midnight: when one stopped at

The station house up top, the other docked at the street,
Underneath a Roman arch. And then the slow descent
Into blight and hock, the grandees making tracks

As the slumlords carved up the lots, downtown down
For the count, white flight, and the end of the line
The summer when man first walked on the moon.

Now it's just for fun: philanthropic angels
Have resurrected it, a civic landmark that doubles as
The world's smallest theme park. You can take

A round-trip on a lark, nodding back at the spirits
Hovering on the other benches—they're catching a ride
For old times' sake, recollecting what it was like

To have a body in motion and at rest.
It can't be helped: the going's bumpy,
The windows clatter, there's no keeping still

With all that jouncing, the cable's shivery tension
Coming up through the soles of your feet.
Here is where you could start to get a little funny

In the head: up in the air, neither here nor there.
If you close your eyes, you might be one of them,
A phantom on an errand, a born-again Angeleno.

From *angelos*, a messenger, beings shuttling
Between heaven and earth, putting in their shifts.
Jacob's funicular? Sounds like the perfect setup

For a running gag here in the part of the world
Where legions of funnymen plied their trade.
Once a working stiff, always a working stiff—

It helps to give an epic shrug, eyes rolling
Up to the heavens. And for the nightclub set,
Something blue: *My dame, she's got a complaint*

In the funicular. I says to her, darlink, you ain't
No duchess. You've got to share your seat
With the good people. Just keep wriggling.

So here you are again, back where you began.
Where does it end? There's a fine line between
Having fun with a thing and playing fast and loose.

Funicular, as in fondly peculiar, no longer
Part of the vernacular, a little funereal.
You hang in the balance. That's how it works.

MATCHBOOK HYMN

Ivy, for scaling.
Ice plant, for creeping.
Green shields, green spears.
A family lies sleeping.

New runners, fresh shoots.
Ivy, for screening.
Downslope a man kneels.
Ice plant, for hedging.

Blast-furnace summers.
Tinderbox evenings.
Ivy, for braiding.
Ice plant, for weaving.

Hazy sun, sooty sky.
What's the radio saying?
Ivy and ice plant.
A woman keeps pacing.

A house on a hillside.
Dry annuals flaring.
Ivy, for grasping.
Ice plant, for reaching.

TO THE TRESPASSER

A quiet akin to ruins—
another contracted hillside, another split-level
fretting the gloaming with its naked beams.

The workmen have all gone home.
The blueprints are curled in their tubes.
The tape measure coils in its shell.

And out he comes, like a storybook constable
making the rounds. There, where the staircase
stops short like a halting phrase,

there, where a swallow circles and dips
through the future picture window, he inspects
the premises, he invites himself in.

There he is now: the calculating smacks
of a palm on the joints and rails,
the faint clouds of whispered advice.

For an hour he will own the place.
His glasses will silver over as he sizes up
the quadrant earmarked for the skylight.

Back then, the houses went up in waves.
He called on them all; he slipped through walls.
Sometimes his son had to wait in the car.

So I always know where I can place him
when I want him at one with himself, at ease:
there, in the mortgaged half-light;

there, where pinches of vagrant sawdust
can collect in his cuffs and every doorframe
welcomes his sidelong blue shadow;

anywhere his dimming form can drift at will
from room to room while dinner's going cold—
a perfect stranger, an auditioning ghost.

PATHETIC FALLACY

Yet another naturalized succulent, but not like the rest of the mob.
   No burly stems, no spiny appendages, nothing coarse or vulgar
you could ascribe to its character. It wasn't lusty ground cover,
   it didn't want the run of the place. It grew,
if grow's the word for it, by putting out beads of milky jade,
   chains of overlapping clusters like little bellropes
or Indian braids—but so grindingly, so grudgingly, you'd think
   it was an agony, you suspected it might be sickly,
which may be why those clinging nodes appeared more gray than green,
   ashen or faded like dollar bills gone through the wash.
As instructed, it had been rigged up on a beam, given room to spill
   from its earthenware planter in its own good time,

looked after, watered sparingly, kept in half shade, kept out of
   the wind, out of harm's way—and even then
it was still testy, touchy, almost visibly aggrieved, as if
   it were nursing some unpardonable wrong going back
to the days when man swung down from the trees. One way or another,
   its dignity had been injured, stung to the quick:
maybe it was smarting over the common name some nurseryman
   pinned on it, dead-on as a sibling crack or playground taunt—
donkey tail, burro tail, try saying it without a smirk—
   mortified to be tagged as ornery when anyone could see
it was simply exercising a fine restraint, refusing to be rushed.
   It was that sensitive, I tell you. Brush past it

too casually, and half a year's strained labor would snap off, a sorry
   litter of teardrop segments like tiny sour grapes
strewn at your feet. Raise your voice, or just stare at it too hard,
   and I swear it would go to pieces. I have the feeling

the poor thing would flinch at any cutting word or abject thought
　　ever to pass under that roof. You have to ache for it,
dangling there exposed in its fistful of soil, shivering on its hook
　　any time a door would slam, a tread tattoo the stair.
O flesh and blood of mine, is there nowhere it could have flourished
　　in our midst, storing up its juices, groping its way downward
knot by chafing knot? Is there nothing remorse will finally stop at,
　　no lash of reproach we can ever spare our mulish hearts?

PROCRUSTEAN

There are other terms we are supposed to use now,
And even then I'm sure compassionate souls
Tiptoed around that abominable epithet
With excruciating tact, letting slip no allusion

That wasn't an exquisitely roundabout euphemism.
So if I say it now, rolling it over my tongue
In all its stunning, gristly backwardness,
You need to understand that I was so unformed then

I wouldn't have known a hunchback if I met one.
The expression meant nothing, no more than spinster
Stood for anything, though she was that too,
A middle-aged woman living with her mother

Not far from the college where she worked with my mom.
But understand, I had no inkling, it just now hits me
How unmistakable it was, how gossips and creeps
Must have been flapping their jaws behind her back

Perhaps just moments after she'd shuffle past,
Swifter than you'd think for one so crooked and bent.
Impossible to miss: the curvature of her spine
Was that pronounced and advanced, the awful torque

Was only getting worse with age, the specialists
Can do nothing to arrest it, the crowbar won't let up . . .
And though you'd hope that would suffice for mortal torment,
I'm here to tell you there were other complications:

A speech impediment, her few halting sentences
Slurred and husky, hard for a kid to catch;
Something seriously amiss with her eyesight,
Lids permanently locked in a stuporlike droop;

A skin condition, some kind of cankered rash
Flaring up her neck, her finger webbing red and pinched.
And to get the full effect, you need to imagine
A women's department of physical education,

A locker-room matron issuing towels and gym socks
To the coltish young things who frisked in to change
For volleyball practice and fitness classes,
Some in tennis whites, some wriggling into leotards

To take my mother's course in modern dance.
If you believed yourself kindhearted and upright,
Here was a tragic figure for you, so crushed
Beneath the world's heel you knew it had to be a test—

And though I know her to be eminently levelheaded,
I think my mother was acting on some queer hunch
When she asked her son if he would rally awhile
With this colleague of hers, as a personal favor.

Painful to look back on now, wrenching to behold—
Almost as if a half-remembered myth had come to life
And a pitiless spirit were taking a twisted pleasure
In mortifying the flesh. What I mean to say is,

The balls came rocketing back so furiously
I knew I was in for a terrible thrashing,
Her backstroke was so heavy with expert slice
I sometimes whiffed and erupted in an ugly curse.

So if I say I want to see her plainly now,
A woman with a hump, a crone before her time,
Who if she is still living is probably bedridden,
Procrustes' pride and joy, broken on the rack,

Try to understand that when it came time
For the traditional handclasp at the net,
There was fur on my tongue, her grip was strong,
And for a moment I thought she'd never let go.

CAUTIONARY TALE

Star of stage and screen, the inspired narrator
Whistled through his teeth as the blizzard raged on.
Then he hissed—that was another arctic blast

Rounding on the little house, shivering its timbers.
Or maybe it was just the pitted surface of the disc.
You played that cut so much it bristled and spit:

The grooves would crunch like crusts of ice underfoot.
Or was that some clever rasp from deep in his throat
Whenever a fresh load of kindling flared up?

Of all the fables on that record, all those yarns
From other lands, this is the only one that's left
A lasting mark—maybe the ice helped to preserve it.

Never mind the frazzled palm outside your room,
The lizards scuffling in the dusty scorch of brush.
The winter could not have been more bitter—

Just listen to the dice clatter of those teeth,
Just think how desperate you'd have to be to sink
Your life savings into an enormous furnace,

A cast-iron monster you'd have to stoke
Around the clock, feeding its feverish ruckus
Anything that burns, even as it roars for more.

Great lungfuls of breath forced out in harsh spurts,
A guttural rumble, lips brushing the mic—
There went the woodpile like so many toothpicks,

There goes the last of the oaken bookshelves
With a gasp in a gout of dragonish smoke.
Or was it an heirloom cedar chest? Certain details

Elude you now, some of this you could be making up.
But not the part when the poor devil seizes his hatchet
(Here's where the huddled townsfolk start to cluck)

And sets about prizing off his shutters and fence slats—
Nails shrieking in falsetto, lion bellows from the oven—
Then with a war whoop clambers up on the roof . . .

When did it turn into a story you tell about yourself?
You hit on a grand plan, you bust your hump,
But you are heedless or luckless, take your pick,

And the next thing you know there are ashes
In your mouth, and that's your fitful heart, all right,
Biting into the silence as you play it all back.

RELIC

Ripped away yet intact—
the orderly bristling
   in the shape of a cup

still holding fast, still
   tight-wound and finespun,
all slick with the wet

   right there on a bookshelf—
here was hard proof
   chaff has its own life,

lashed into place,
   rife with the stuff
of craft and chance

   (candyfoil, shredded
Christmas ribbon, legible bits
   of an ancient *Star-News*),

and there it was still,
   right in our midst
through the course of events,

   the alas and alack,
the ever after of it,
   our handsbreadth of

lasting happenstance
   plucked from the wrack
of windfall eucalyptus,

still giving off
that gummy whiff
    of a medicine chest,

as if it once held
    our ration of a potion
or a serum

    in its tangle of
gleanings: abracadabra,
    the works, the goods

(broomstraw, kitestring,
    fine reddish glints
of the youngest's hair),

    a scoop of our
small world, half full,
    half empty, all there.

HORSE CHESTNUTS

Then all at once the prickly cases split
And my coatpockets bulge with touchstone keepsakes.
Let me try to explain. Within earshot of the overpass
I took riding lessons: the long-suffering mares
Broke out in a smoking sweat as I logged my circuits,
An oily glow that left them looking varnished.
They'd seen my kind before: high strung, quick to spook.
The stable paid a girl my age to hose them down
And curry them. Her skin was coppery from all that sun.
Her nipples were brown circles she didn't bother to disguise.
No, please—there's more. There's the back of the guitar
I curled my body around every day for two semesters:
Glossy auburn whorls streaked with bands of resin,
Heartwood tints a woman once compared to the raw honey
And hard cider of her childhood. She'd grown up on a farm.
The manager knew a rube when he saw one: he made straight
For the window display where the upscale models floated
In overlapping succession, like phases of the moon.
Classical lessons, finger exercises: you had to move
Your hands clawlike, crabwise, up and down the neck.
In the nightspot where my inscrutable instructor
Played a regular weekend gig, the close-set tabletops
Were redwood burls, and the scrolled mahogany chairs
Were inlaid with slivers of abalone that would gleam
In the modish dimness like the flawless crescents
Of his nails. Suites and preludes: I'd watch the women
Watching him. He was a clotheshorse and a rake,
And it's possible I thought some of his touch
Had to rub off. It's possible those lacquered mares
I urged around the ring embodied some unconscious wish

On my parents' part to burnish a vision of their past:
A faintly recollected golden age when L.A.'s ranches
Outnumbered cloverleaf ramps and blacktop lots.
It's one thing after another, a winnowing motion,
A rivering grain, the mind never coming to rest,
Finding itself wanting. An able friend of mine strips
Battered chests of drawers down to the original wood—
Century-old walnut, chestnut, cherry, cedar, oak—
Then strokes on stains that lock in cherished highlights.
He's made a living that way. Sometimes we talk
While he works: women, our folks, the weather.
I no longer ride; I barely play; I couldn't fit out
A cabinet to save my life. I'm only trying to explain
How it happens that your man takes so much longer
Getting home this time of year, when the spiked capsules
Crack at last and riddle the shaggy park grasses
With the finished windfall sheen of horse chestnuts.

NETTLES OF THE FIELD

STINGING (*URTICA DIOICA*)

Look me up again: I burn.
Who wants to fester, who'd like to learn
How flesh is grass all over again?
You'll rue the day you brushed by me.
Can pain be love? I love to burn.
The sun loves pain or else why would
I shoot up rife in the summer woods?
There's no right way to rub me, friend:
I'll leave you raw, I'll leave you red,
Blistered, rankled, smarting, singed.
One stray touch—that's all it takes.
I don't even need to break the skin.
This is not ire, understand—
Pain's my pleasure, a sweet release.
I know my place. I ask you this:
What balm or simple under the sun
Cures anyone of their innocence?
I hear you swashing through my glen,
Where light turns leaves into licks of flame.
Give me scorched earth. I love to burn.

FALSE (*BOEHMARIA CYLINDRICA*)

Now turn the page: I blend
Right in. Toothed leaves, bright stems
In the dog-day scrub by the fire road—
Is this not innately nettlesome?

Come, come: don't flinch. All's well that ends.
I'm nothing if not the forgiving kind.
I mean no harm. I give you my word.
You can do with me what you will.
Live and let live is what I say:
If you don't ask, I'll never tell.
Bend closer still, and then you'll see
I'm not the one you think I am.
Is that your heart racing? Are you getting warm?
I know, I know: you've been here before
And I can tell you've had your fill
Of looking sharp and hanging fire.
Fear not: no matter what you feel
I won't let on that it's for real.
It's true: I'm false. It's my saving grace.
I'm false: it's true. That's why I'm safe.

THREE SONGS IN THE MASK OF PAN

I

What else was there to do?
    I yanked her up with my fists.
I was still breathing hard.
    She was still warm from the chase.
It nearly took forever
    To get the pitches right:
The current lapped my haunches;
    My rib cage went in and out.
I couldn't keep good time.
    I copped no killer licks.
It was as if she gasped when
    I ran her over my lips.

II

What would you have me do?
    I am no guitar god.
Nymphs never fall at my feet.
    My fingering is crude.
I couldn't jump her bones.
    She left me grasping air.
My playing was like panting;
    My mouth was still on fire.
But grief is a kind of riff
    And ragged stalks can be tuned.
My rib cage went out and in.
    That's how the blues were born.

III

You think I had a clue?
   I poured my poor guts out.
An ibis broke for cover
   As if it heard a ghost.
My playing is a sobbing
   All up and down her stops.
Sometimes my strains can sound like
   A creature with two backs.
Panic can give you a rush.
   Rapmasters, sample this:
Your breath saws back and forth
   Until there comes a voice.

RED FIGURE

I. BELL KRATER: DEATH OF AKTAION

One has already got him by the throat.
He is about to crumple into a heap,
One arm flailing, but there's nothing to grasp—
No other goddess has a dog in this scrap,
And if one did, it's already too late.

Now he's the naked one: you can hear him gasp
As one sinks its mouth into his reeling trunk.
Swallow hard, my fellows. Drink up, drink up!
There will be no little death for this dumb beast.

Enough already, or so you would think,
But the huntress isn't finished with him yet.
She's drawing back a feathered shaft, point-blank,
Still seeing red, lest there be some mistake:
No bathing beauty, nobody's mate.

II. AMPHORA: RHAPSODE

This one throws his head back like a rocker,
Pouring out his soul, jamming on his lyre.
He's going platinum. He knows his Homer
Like he knows his heartbeat, only better.
No reason is in him. So it is written.
Strophe after strophe, something molten
Coursing through his system, something golden.

Sing it, brother. You are inspired.
The honeyed muse is brandishing your body.
The painter saw to it you sprang from the fire
By utterance possessed, beside yourself, spotlit
On the vessel's pitch-black, a blaze of glory.
And what they say is true, for a poet
Is a light and winged thing, and holy.

PSALM FOR A SUGARHOUSE

Here in the creak and the dark,
Take heart and mouth your clouds:
Be it ever so ice locked,
You're ringed by maple woods.

Let that be your pure thought
Here in the numb and the gloom:
The sap will answer the knock,
The taproot calls up the stem.

Hunker and let your heart feast
Here in the stark and the bleak:
No word need cross your lips,
There is no switch to throw,
Be it ever so bone wracked,
One mild snap primes the flow.

Here in the stammer and shiver,
Let this cast your lot:
In all the leafless hollows
The fuse is already lit,
If the mercury's a blood drop,
The pressure's building up . . .

Be it ever so dumbstruck
Here in the grip of the grim,
Sweet is the open secret
Here on the tip of your tongue.

ROGUE MOSS

Emboldened now, no longer earthbound,
No more shrinking into the shadowy lee
As if plain sight were a station
Not for a moment to be contemplated,
Shunning attention, renouncing ambition.

Finespun still, but with a newfound fervor—
None of that tremulous aversion
To exposure, that fanatical clinging
To fastidious humility, which is itself
A form of overweening vanity.

Lovely the seeping cranny, sweet
The rift where the mortar gives, the fissure
Shivering through the loose garden slate—
Possible to hold fast to all this
Obliging neglect and still aspire.

Aroused, impelled, sensing the main chance
At last: the boxy cinder-block garage
Put up who knows when, no pitch
To that slab roof, rainwater pooling
For days on end, tar paper all rot and tatter.

Flaring this morning, distinctly glimmering,
First thing one spots from the porch upslope—
Fetching woven stuff, a living velvet sheen
Stealing across that blistered surface
Like a desert prophecy come to pass.

Still emblematic of all that's delicate,
Everything chastened and constrained,
But with a steelier glint, as if to offer proof
That here is how another nature might yet
Make itself felt: ascendant, rampant, plush.

NAIL BROTH

Rusty, twisted: scrounge one from a scrap-heap plank.
How long did you say you've been down on your luck?

Rasping groan, out it comes: crude thing, fanglike.
Exactly how low are you intending to sink?

Lockjaw's no picnic. Look sharp: don't get pricked.
Wouldn't it be simpler to stick with the tin cup?

There's an old crone I know—a classic skinflint.
Doesn't she ever get wise to your act?

When you live by your wits, you go with your gut.
How do you sleep with such sham in your heart?

Root cellar, spice larder, bomb shelter, ice box.
Does it really help when you smack your lips?

Stir like you mean it. Keep up the sweet talk.
Do you know in your bones when she's ready to crack?

Steam up the panes. A round stone also works.
Are you trying to say you'll do whatever it takes?

NOTES AND SOURCES

CHIMERICAL

Captain James Cook's vessel, the *Endeavour*, put in for repairs on the northeastern coast of Australia in June 1770. The ship's chief naturalist was Joseph Banks, later president of the Royal Society. Vanessa Collingridge, *Captain Cook: A Legacy Under Fire* (Guilford, Conn.: Lyons Press, 2002); Patrick O'Brian, *Joseph Banks: A Life* (Chicago: University of Chicago Press, 1997); Harriet Ritvo, *The Platypus and the Mermaid and Other Figments of the Classifying Imagination* (Cambridge: Harvard University Press, 1997).

A COLONIAL EPITAPH ANNOTATED

Thomas C. Mann and Janet Greene, *Over Their Dead Bodies: Yankee Epitaphs and History* (Brattleboro, Vt.: Stephen Greene Press, 1962).

EULOGY FOR AN ANCHORITE

Born Karl Kehrle in what was then the kingdom of Württemberg in southern Germany, Brother Adam entered the English Benedictine monastery of Buckfast Abbey in 1910 at the age of twelve. He died on September 1, 1996. The Monticola is a strain of honeybee native to the Mount Kilimanjaro region. *American Bee Journal* (October 1996).

INQUEST

Brian Innes, "Instruments of Torture," chapter 8 in *The History of Torture* (New York: St. Martin's Press, 1998).

THUMBNAIL SKETCH OF THE TULIPMANIA

My original source for much of the lore surrounding the speculative market in tulips in 1630s Holland was the chapter "The Tulipomania" in Charles Mackay's *Extraordinary Popular Delusions and the Madness of Crowds,* originally published in London in 1841. The poem also draws on "The Bitter Scent of Tulips," a chapter in Zbigniew Herbert's *Still Life with a Bridle* (New York: Ecco Press, 1991), a collection of "essays and apocryphas" on Dutch art.

MASTERS OF THE FLORILEGIUM
The two quotations and certain details on medieval florilegia are drawn from Jean Leclercq, O.S.B., *The Love of Learning and the Desire for God: A Study of Monastic Culture,* translated by Catharine Misrahi (New York: Fordham University Press, 1961).

FROM A BURBANK CATALOGUE
Luther Burbank (1849–1926) was the most celebrated horticulturalist of his day, hailed at the height of his renown as a "plant wizard" and credited with developing hundreds of hybrid fruits, vegetables, and flowers. He ran a thriving mail-order business from his nursery in Santa Rosa, California, and in 1893 issued the first of many catalogues advertising his seeds and bulbs, *New Creations in Fruits and Flowers.*

APHRODITE'S MOUSETRAP
John Bartram was appointed the King's Botanist for the North American colonies by George III in 1765. Thomas P. Slaughter, *The Natures of John and William Bartram* (New York: Alfred A. Knopf, 1996); William A. Niering and Nancy C. Olmstead, *The Audubon Society Field Guide to North American Wildflowers, Eastern Region* (New York: Alfred A. Knopf, 1979).

BALLADE OF THE GOLDEN ARM
Stephen Kinzer, "Bokonbayeva Journal: God of Birds, but Scourge of Foxes and Badgers," *New York Times,* November 4, 1999.

SOURCE
Fray Antonio de la Calancha (1584–1654) was born of Spanish parents in Chuquisaca, a mining center in upper Peru, now part of Bolivia. The poem's italicized passages are drawn from an excerpt of his two-volume history of his Augustine order in Peru that appeared in *The Golden Land: An Anthology of Latin American Folklore in Literature* (New York: Alfred A. Knopf, 1948), edited and translated by Harriet De Onís. A few remarks from De Onís's preface may be useful as an additional gloss: "His lifetime work was a history of his order in Peru, *Crónica moralizada del Orden de San Agustín en el Perú, con sucesos ejemplares de esta monarquía,* the first volume of which was published in Barcelona in 1638, and the second in Lima in 1653. But rather than the orderly, dull account its title would indicate, it is a most entertaining rag-bag of fact, gossip, superstition, and miracle . . . All who have studied the history of the Incan empire have marvelled

at how they could have built their imposing temples and monuments, often transporting the materials hundreds of miles, without knowing the use of the wheel; and how they could have kept full records of their past without possessing an alphabet. In this description of the *quipus* Fray Antonio gives a fascinating account of how they employed a most intricate system of knotted threads as a substitute for writing."

ODE TO WILLIAM WELLS
William Charles Wells (1757–1817) published his "Essay on Dew" in 1814. Loren Eiseley, *Darwin's Century: Evolution and the Men Who Discovered It* (New York: Anchor Books, 1961).

NEW WORLD SUTRAS
The Sanskrit word *sutra* literally means "thread" or "line." In its more familiar religious sense, it originally referred to a pithy verse or aphorism or a collection of such utterances. As one of the principal modes of both Vedic and Buddhist scripture, the sutra evolved into an eclectic medium for teachings on ritual law and the conduct of life, composed with an eye to gnomic economy and mnemonic resonance. In that spirit, these pieces occasionally borrow phrases and locutions from their framing personages that seemed to me to aspire to the condition of proverbial expression.

HOUDINI SUTRA
The first stanza is part of a sentence taken from the notebooks of Harry Houdini (Ehrich Weiss). From "Houdini's Double Box Mystery" in Walter B. Gibson's *Houdini's Escapes and Magic* (New York: Funk and Wagnalls, 1976).

WALLENDA SUTRA
Karl Wallenda (1905–78) was the patriarch of the Flying Wallendas, the "first family" of high-wire aerialists. He fell to his death while performing a tightrope walk between two buildings in San Juan, Puerto Rico. The poem appropriates a motto attributed to Wallenda that has come down in several versions: "Life is being on the wire; everything else is just waiting."

GREAT STONE FACE SUTRA
The title refers to the well-known press moniker for Buster Keaton, who was said to have perfected his trademark deadpan expression as a child performing in his family vaudeville act, the Three Keatons.

IGNATZ SUTRA

The Krazy Kat comic strip was the creation of George Herriman (1880–1944) and ran in one form or another in Hearst newspapers from 1913 to Herriman's death. Aficionados will know that the strip's running gag was Krazy's unrequited love for Ignatz Mouse, who routinely pelted his hapless admirer with well-aimed bricks. (For C., in memoriam.)

SATCHMO SUTRA

Louis Armstrong's landmark studio recordings with his ensembles the Hot Five and the Hot Seven are by common consent the foundational documents of modern jazz. The poem's first line is an apocryphal phrase widely attributed to him.

BAMBINO SUTRA

Yankee Stadium opened in 1923. It is not known which press wag promptly dubbed it the House That Ruth Built.

DOUBLE ELEPHANT FOLIO SUTRA

The original four-volume edition of John James Audubon's *The Birds of America* (1827–38) was published as a "double elephant folio," at the time the largest format for bound collections of prints or engravings. Audubon insisted on those dimensions (roughly two feet by three feet) in keeping with his ambition to draw all his specimens to scale. The great auk and the Carolina parakeet were nearing extinction when he completed his work.

ZOOPRAXISCOPE SUTRA

The zoopraxiscope is the name the pioneering action photographer Eadweard Muybridge (1830–1904) gave to his projection apparatus for viewing sequences of slides that produced the illusion of motion, thus foreshadowing modern cinematography. It was a complicated technical gizmo based on earlier persistence-of-vision devices such as the magic lantern and the zoetrope (also known as the wheel of life). Muybridge's experiments with capturing split-second exposures began in 1878, when the California railroad magnate Leland Stanford commissioned him to photograph his champion trotter, Occident, to settle the dispute over whether all four hooves of a running horse ever leave the ground at once. (Verdict: they do.) He later undertook an exhaustive series of "motion studies" that was published under the title *Animal Locomotion* (1887) and in several abridged editions.

FUNICULAR

Angels Flight Railway: Grand Re-Opening Celebration Commemorative Book (Los Angeles: Angels Flight Railway Company, 1996).

RED FIGURE

The closing lines are taken from Plato's *Ion* (Lane Cooper translation, 1938).

ABOUT THE AUTHOR

David Barber is the poetry editor of *The Atlantic.* His first collection of poems, *The Spirit Level,* received the Terrence Des Pres Prize from TriQuarterly Books.